IDENTIFY HER

Identify Her

P.E.A.R.L.S of Wisdom that Build Confidence and Help Young Girls Walk in Purpose

JESSICA HARDY

ISBN: :979-8-9892806-6-7

Published by 120 Publishing House.
5240 Prairie View Way,
Wesley Chapel FL 33545
www.120dayspublishing.com

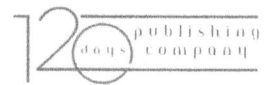

P
Powerful perspective and
Permission to Pursue

E
Embrace the right relationships

a
Amplify your authentic voice

R
Realizing you are a Child of God/Revelation
of who God is

L
Love of the Father

S
Success in your story

GET YOUR FREE GIFT

Hey friend, you are not alone on this journey. I want to connect with you and help you overcome every mountain that has come to hinder your progress towards healing. So I have a special gift for you. Simply click the link or visit the link below, for access to your digital resource. Use this journal daily to take the next steps needed to truly embrace who you are.

YOU CAN GET A COPY BY VISITING

https://thejessicahardy.com

Dedication

This book is dedicated to those who are struggling with rejection, to those who struggle with abandonment, to those who struggle with low self worth and even those that feel overlooked. May the pages in this book help you overcome those struggles and lead you to the one that can heal.

CONTENTS

Acknowledgments

This book would not have made it from my head to paper if it was not for a few people that assisted in some way. First, I would like to thank my husband for his ongoing support and sacrifice when it comes to me and my endeavors. I don't take anything you do lightly and I'm extremely grateful for you.

I also would like to acknowledge the people that have aided in my transformation through their obedience to God and those people are Minister Nikki Spencer, Teresa Veney, Dr. Karen Bethea and my counselor Tanya Manywethers. The teachings and encouragement that was extended to me through what seemed to be the toughest moments in my life was nothing short of a blessing. Thank you for pouring into me and speaking life into my future.

A very special Thank you to Triana "Bunny" Flemming for your encouragement and genuine support over the past few months, it has not gone unnoticed. Also, thanks for connecting me to the best manuscript midwife there is, Taushauna Burrel.

Last but not least, thank you to Taushauna Burrel and 120 Publishing House for making my book writing and publishing process seamless and with ease.

Preface

This book was birthed from a place of profound brokenness—a space where emotional pain, though harrowing, unfolded as an immense blessing. The trials of rejection, abandonment, and being misunderstood pushed me to depend on God more intensely than ever before. In surrendering fully and casting all my cares upon Him, as 1 Peter 5:7 instructs, emerged a narrative designed to guide and empower adolescent girls. It's a call to lean on and establish a true relationship with God, to identify who they are in Christ before life's challenges try to shape their self-perception.

Imagine us as oysters, and our life's challenges as the grains of sand that invade our peace. Just as an oyster covers these irritants with layers of nacre to form pearls, God envelops our troubles, transforming them into testimonials of His grace. The formation of a pearl is not instantaneous—it takes years. Similarly, our spiritual growth and development are processes nurtured over time, through trials and tribulations that God uses to refine us.

Pearls symbolize the rare, the beautiful, and the resilient. They encapsulate wisdom and the transformative power of life's pressures. Most captivating to me is their symbolism of strength and resilience, qualities bestowed upon us as we navigate through life's tempests under God's protective grace.

This book stands as a testament that we, too, can become pearls, masterfully crafted by God. He has taken the fragmented pieces of my past, healed them, and granted me the wisdom to offer guidance. This narrative aims not only to recount my journey but to equip you with the understanding that early recognition of your identity in Christ can profoundly influence your life's trajectory.

In the following chapters, I share the P.E.A.R.L.S— principles that have anchored me. Missing the opportunity to grasp these pearls could mean missing out on the essence of what God intends for you. Through my experiences laid out on these pages, I aim to demonstrate the significance of embracing every facet of your journey, including the challenges. My hope is that by sharing my story, you will see how adversities are often the fertile soil for discovering and embracing your true identity in God.

Let's embark on this journey together, not just to read another story, but to uncover the radiant pearl God intends each of us to become. Through this discovery, may you find the courage to own and celebrate your identity, knowing that with God, every aspect of your story is purposeful and powerful.

Introduction

To: God's Precious Pearl,

Congratulations on beginning this transformative journey to discover your identity in Christ. This process, filled with its highs and lows, is not just about growth—it's about revelation and reaching deep into the heart of who you are meant to be. Every step, every challenge, and every victory is crafting a unique story designed especially for you, one that will resonate with others who walk similar paths. Your experience is invaluable; imagine being the guiding light for someone who traverses the same trials you've conquered. Isn't that a journey worth undertaking?

My own path was fraught with questions and trials that tested my faith and forged my character. Growing up as the often-overlooked daughter of divorced parents, with a father frequently away in military service, I wrestled with feelings of abandonment and insignificance. Sundays at church were a constant in my life, yet outside those sacred walls, I grappled with rejection, comparison, and a profound lack of self-worth. These struggles weren't just emotional hurdles; they shaped decisions that led to tangible losses—time, opportunities, and peace.

This book is born from a deep desire to spare you those detours. It's here to offer you the pearls of wisdom I gathered along the way—insights that I wish had been imparted to me earlier. You will find them at the end of most chapters known as "identity check" points. These are to ensure you are able to find your true north at the end of each chapter that outlines the biggest trial I faced while discovering who I was in Christ. It's a literal trial :-)

As we go on this journey together, you will learn how to navigate life's challenges by fostering a genuine relationship with God. This isn't just about finding out who you are; it's about embracing the divine purpose crafted just for you.

Imagine having the confidence to stand firm in your uniqueness, to voice your truth boldly, and to know, without a shadow of a doubt, that you are fearfully and wonderfully made. That knowledge, that foundation in Christ, changes everything. You are a child of God—cherished, seen, and destined for greatness.

As you turn these pages, you'll gain tools and insights that will guide you through the complexities of life and into the clarity of your divine identity. Get ready to uncover the essence of who you are, as we journey together to not just identify you, but to celebrate and affirm the incredible person God has created you to be.

Sincerely,

Jessica Hardy

CHAPTER 1:

The Sermon That Changed Everything

"**A**re you kidding me right now? How is this lady reading my entire life like a book?" Tears streamed down my face as I listened, spellbound and slightly shell-shocked. Minister Nikki wasn't just delivering a sermon; it felt more like she was conducting a funeral—and something inside me was definitely dying but, strangely, something else was fiercely coming to life.

On that pivotal Sunday, it felt like both Big Jessica and little Jessica sat side-by-side on that church pew, undergoing a profound healing. A healing that whispered courage into the depths of my spirit, nudging me toward the daunting yet liberating steps I needed to take. It was as if Minister Nikki spoke directly to the little girl inside me, the one who'd been hiding behind adult decisions and responsibilities, coaxing her out into the healing light of God's love.

Hi, I'm Jessica, if you hadn't figured that out yet, and this is more than just a recount of my life—it's the story of how God used every twist and drama to help me break away from the old versions of myself. This is about how I discovered who I really was in Him, which allowed me to become the best version of myself.

I grew up in a single-family home with my mother and brother. To the outside observer, my childhood might have seemed pretty standard and stable. There was always food on the table, clothes on my back, and a roof over my head. Yet, beneath that veneer of stability were layers of unspoken struggles—rejection, low self-worth, and a profound sense of not belonging.

These invisible battles didn't just complicate my childhood; they followed me into adulthood, shaping decisions and relationships in ways I didn't fully understand until that life-altering sermon. That day, as Minister Nikki shared her own story of letting go and starting anew, it was as though she was narrating mine. She talked about the courage it took to step away from a toxic relationship with the father of her child—a narrative that mirrored my own.

It wasn't just a sermon; it was a wake-up call. She spoke of healing and new beginnings in such a personal way that it pierced right through to the heart of my own pain and aspirations. The way she had to escape to rediscover herself resonated deeply. "She had to get away," Nikki revealed, speaking of her own journey to sever the ties that bound her to a life of unfulfilled promises and unrealized potential.

I sat there, the hard pew under me, feeling every word like a weight lifting off my chest. It sparked a revelation, a hot, tearful revelation that it was time for me to do the same. If she could reset her life's narrative, why couldn't I? The idea that I didn't have to force a fantasy but could actually step into a new reality was both frightening and exhilarating.

I bought the sermon on CD, because I knew this was a message I'd need to hear again. Listening to it repeatedly, the words became a mantra for change.

As I drove home from church that day, my mind was abuzz with the possibilities of what letting go truly meant. The life I had clung to, primarily out of fear and a misplaced sense of loyalty, was suddenly up for renegotiation.

I realized that the situationship with my daughter's father, which had been a comfortable yet uninspiring and unfulfilling fixture in my life, had to end. It had become clear that I was holding on to a semblance of family for our daughter, much like the two-parent home I never experienced but always envied.

Determined to embrace the life God intended for me, I decided to set boundaries, an action I'd never been bold enough to take. Despite his dismissive laughter when I told him things needed to change, I felt a surge of empowerment. For the first time, I chose my well-being, guided by a newfound faith rather than the fear of conflict or rejection.

But setting boundaries was just the beginning. They were tested, trampled, and disregarded, leading to a whirlwind of custody disputes and legal battles I never anticipated. This confrontation with the court system was daunting, yet it forced me to confront the people-pleasing tendencies that had dictated much of my life's direction.

This chapter, this sermon, wasn't just a turning point; it was the start of a journey to rediscover my worth, to redefine my relationships, and to realign my life with God's purpose. It taught me that breaking free from the past involves more than just physical separation; it requires a spiritual awakening and the courage to confront deeply ingrained fears and falsehoods.

And so, this book is for anyone who's ever felt stuck, misunderstood, or undervalued. It's for those who are tired of playing roles that don't fit and wearing masks that hide their true faces. It's a testament to the transformative power of faith, the liberating truth of God's love, and the incredible journey to becoming the person you were truly meant to be.

IDENTITY CHECK: UNLOCKING YOUR P.E.A.R.L.S OF POWER

Quote:

"No matter what you do in life, someone may have an issue with it, but you have to continue to walk confidently and boldly in the things you believe in, especially the things of God."

End this chapter with a moment to reflect and activate the pearls of wisdom you've gathered. Let's polish these pearls with some focused action:

1. **Pinpoint the Issue:** Identify a specific challenge you're facing right now. Is it related to self-doubt, maintaining boundaries, or perhaps managing expectations? Naming it is the first step to taming it.

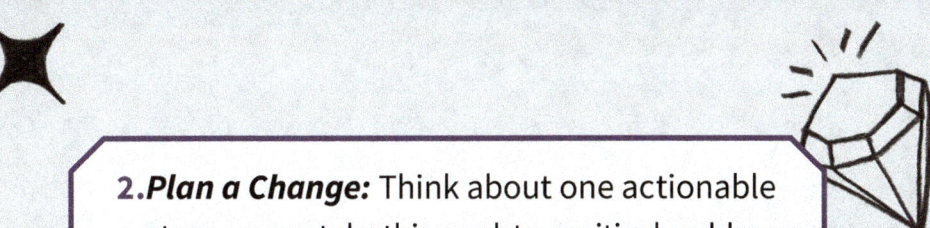

2.**Plan a Change:** Think about one actionable step you can take this week to positively address this issue. Whether it's speaking up about your needs, setting a boundary, or simply giving yourself permission to fail, write it down.

3. **Proceed with Purpose:** Commit to your action for the next week. Track your feelings and any changes in your situation daily. This isn't just about overcoming a challenge; it's about evolving through it.

Reflect on how these steps help you move closer to your true identity, fostering a stronger, more resilient you. Each step you take is crafting the unique pearl of your life's story.

CHAPTER 2:

Church Talks

"Are you kidding me right now?" That's what I think to myself as I settle into what feels more like a confession booth than a therapist's office. The soothing scent of lavender fills the air, a gentle reminder that it's okay to relax. But can I really relax when I'm about to bare my soul? "Hey, I'm here because I'm in a situation that hurts and I realized I have low confidence." Sound familiar? Maybe you've been there too, standing at the threshold of change, scared but ready.

Let's get real for a moment. How often do we admit our deepest fears to ourselves, let alone to someone else? It's tough, right? As I began my sessions, I learned the power of honesty—not just in what I told my counselor, but in what I admitted to myself. It's like unpacking a suitcase after a long trip; you don't really know what's in there until you open it up.

Now, think about your own life. What are the issues you've duct-taped shut? What would it mean for you to unpack them, maybe even in a sand tray session like I did? **The sand tray exercise involved a simple tray filled with sand in which various figures and objects could be placed and arranged. My counselor used it as a metaphorical playing field for my mind, where each figure represented different aspects of my personal narrative. I was asked to choose figures that represented people, emotions, or significant events in my life and position them in the sand in a way that reflected my current feelings and relationships. This tactile experience was not just creative play; it was a profound way of visualizing and confronting the components of my psyche in a safe, controlled environment.**

Imagine arranging figures in the sand—how would you position them to represent your current challenges?

Through my counseling, I realized how much of our self-worth gets tangled up in past pains. We traced my steps back to childhood, uncovering events that shaped my self-view and my relationships. It wasn't easy, but it was enlightening. What about you? Can you trace any of your current struggles back to earlier chapters of your life? How does recognizing these roots help you understand your present?

One powerful tool my counselor introduced me to was affirmations. Standing in front of the mirror each morning, I'd say, "I am enough, just as I am." Sounds simple, but it's revolutionary. What words do you need to hear? Maybe write them down now, or find a verse that speaks to you. Psalm 139:14 is a great place to start: "I praise you, for I am fearfully and wonderfully made."

Parallel to my therapy, I found a second home in Joshua's Journey, a young adult ministry at my church. Here's where the magic happened—not just in healing but in growing through serving others. We often think we need to be fully healed before we can help others, but what if reaching out is part of the healing process? Have you ever experienced this?

In Joshua's Journey, not only did I learn to pray and worship in a way that connected deeply with God, but I also discovered the joy of serving. From group home visits to cooking sessions, every act of service taught me something about myself and God's grace. What opportunities do you have to serve in your community? How might stepping out to help others also bring healing to your own life?

As I reflect on my journey of counseling and church involvement, I see it wasn't just about overcoming challenges; it was about discovering my identity as a Child of God. So, I invite you to consider: What steps can you take today to start uncovering your true identity? Maybe it's joining a community, starting therapy, or simply sitting in quiet reflection.

Remember, every step you take is a part of the extraordinary journey God has planned for you. Are you ready to take that step?

IDENTITY CHECK:
"DO YOU KNOW YOU?"

1. *Self-Discovery Writing:*
   - **What are your likes and dislikes?**
     Take a moment to jot down things that bring joy to your life and those that don't.
     - ○ **Identify Your Gifts**:
       What are you naturally good at? List some talents or skills that define you.

2. *Affirmation Challenge:*
   - **Facing Challenges with Faith**:
     Reflect on the issues identified in Chapter 1's exercise. Choose three affirmations or Bible verses that address these issues. Examples to consider:
     - ○ *"I am fearfully and wonderfully made."* – Psalm 139:14
     - ○ *"I am enough, just as I am."*
     - ○ *"I am loved by God, no matter my past."*

- ○ **21-Day Affirmation Practice**:
  Write each chosen affirmation or
  verse on a notecard. Focus on one
  affirmation, reciting it daily for 21
  days before moving to the next. This
  practice is designed to reshape your
  thoughts and strengthen your spirit.

3. **Daily Time with God**:
   - **Schedule Spiritual Reflection**: Set a
     specific time each day for prayer and
     reflection. Use this time to connect deeply
     with God, focusing on your journey and
     His presence in your life.

   - **Reflective Practice**: During your daily
     time, reflect on past challenges you've
     overcome. Thank Him for His sovereignty
     and guidance. This practice helps to
     acknowledge His continual presence and
     fosters a deeper connection.

For more resources to support your 21-day
affirmation challenge, visit www.theJessicaHardy.
com. Join a community of seekers and find tools to
help you affirm and grow in your identity in Christ.

CHAPTER 3:

Spiritual Mom

Imagine this: It's early Sunday morning, and I'm nestled in the sound booth at church, surrounded by the familiar hum of electronics and the quiet before the storm of worship. This is where I found my groove, tucked away among dials and monitors, feeling the pulse of the service in every button press. Each CD I duplicated—yes, those round discs that preceded our streaming playlists—carried a sermon that might just change someone's life as it echoed beyond our walls.

Working in this hidden niche, I was paired with Ms. Teresa, a veteran in managing church sound and media, who became my spiritual mom. What's a spiritual mom, you ask? She's someone who nurtures your growth in faith and life, guiding you through challenges not just with advice, but with love, prayer, and scriptures.

As we worked together, our relationship grew from technical tips on sound mixing to life lessons. Ms. Teresa had a knack for storytelling, her words sprinkled with humor and hard truths. One morning, as we were setting up, I confided in her about the struggles I was facing with my daughter's father and the messy court battles that ensued. She listened, her responses seasoned with grace and wisdom, sharing her own similar experiences. This connection was no coincidence; it was a divine setup, providing me with the guidance I needed at just the right time.

The night before my assault charge case was a pivotal moment. My spiritual mom and I sat together, praying and conversing like any other evening. It was then I fully recognized the gift of having her in my life—a true Titus 2 woman who nurtured and guided me through turbulent waters. My counselor and she prepared me as best as they could, instilling in me the strength to call upon God as my vindicator.

The following morning, I walked through the courthouse doors, less intimidated than ever before, bolstered by the peace that surpassed all understanding. As I passed through metal detectors and entered courtroom 1, an unexpected calm settled over me. When my name was called, I approached the podium, and the judge delivered news that would change everything: "The state has decided to Nolle Pros your case." The charges were dropped. Relief washed over me as I walked out, a new trust in God's unwavering presence firmly rooted in my heart. The song *"Won't He Do It"* by Koryn Hawthorne played on the radio as I drove away, tears of joy streaming down my face.

In moments of uncertainty, when outcomes seem foggy and fear looms large, leaning into God's promises brings clarity and peace. Ms. Teresa always reminded me of Isaiah 41:10, which promises God's strength and support. This scripture, once words on a page, became a living, breathing testament to God's faithfulness in my life.

If we are truly going to grow and develop beyond life's emotional, spiritual, or physical issues, spiritual parenting is crucial. Mentoring is something we should actively seek, or be open to when God places us in proximity to our mentors and spiritual parents, often right on time.

Now, let me share with you how you can apply these insights into your own life:

IDENTITY CHECK:

QUOTE:

"I encourage you to follow what God commands in the bible so you can avoid unnecessary situations that are the result of our disobedience to the Father."

- ## REFLECTION
  Think about the spiritual mentors in your life. What have they taught you? How can you apply these lessons to your current challenges?

- ## ACTION
  Write down a scripture that has touched your heart recently. Reflect on its application in your daily life. How can this scripture guide you through current struggles or decisions?

- **CONNECTION**

  Consider the relationships that feed your soul. Do you have a spiritual mentor like Ms. Teresa? If not, seek out someone who can fulfill this role. What qualities would you look for in a spiritual mentor?

- **COMMITMENT**

  Set a daily appointment with yourself to meditate, pray, or simply sit in silence. Use this time to connect deeply with your inner self and God, allowing His peace to calm the chaos of daily life.

Through these steps, not only do you learn about my journey, but you also discover how to navigate your own path with faith and the support of those God places in your life.

CHAPTER 4:

Self-Edification

After navigating the roller coaster of the assault charge and feeling the ground steadying under my feet, i found solace back in an old sanctuary of mine—the local library. Imagine that calming scent of books, each one a gateway to new worlds and insights. There's something inherently peaceful about wandering through library aisles, picking out books that whisper secrets about life and growth.

During this reflective time, i stumbled upon two transformative books: soul detox by craig groeschel and addicted to pain by rainie howard. Each book seemed to reach out to me from the shelves, promising guidance and understanding. Soul detox shed light on cleansing myself of toxic emotions—how timely, right? Meanwhile, addicted to pain offered a mirror into my own struggles, providing a path to heal from the toxic relationships that had clouded my past.

This wasn't just about reading; it was about rediscovering a passion that calmed the chaos that seemed to swirl around court dates and custody battles. These books became my therapists, my guides, and my friends, teaching me crucial lessons about self-worth and the power of healing. They helped me identify with the woman on the cover, a poised appearance masking a torrent of inner turmoil. It was a profound connection, seeing my own polished exterior while grappling with a flood of emotions underneath.

Through addicted to pain, I learned the importance of self-love and setting boundaries. It was like having a big sister in book form, constantly reminding me that I deserved so much more than the scraps of affection I had settled for. This newfound perspective was empowering. For once, I could see toxic behaviors not just as personal failures, but as patterns that I had the power to change.

As I healed, I also leaned heavily into my faith. The bible became a daily source of strength and comfort, especially through plans like "rescue: finding God in life's challenges." Each session tackled emotions from fear to hope, each day feeling like a step forward in a journey of recovery and self-discovery. The idea that questioning "Why me, God?" Could be the start of heal-ing was revolutionary for me. It shifted my perspective from feeling victimized to being proactive in my spiri-tual and emotional recovery.

These readings taught me that knowing better leads to doing better. They expanded my understand-ing of myself and the world around me, equipping me with tools to face whatever the next chapter of life held. And in those quiet moments between the pages, i found not just escape, but real strategies for living a fuller, more grounded life.

Books and faith taught me an invaluable lesson: the chapters of our lives, much like those in our favorite novels, are filled with trials, triumphs, and transforma-tions. Embracing each phase, each lesson, is crucial in crafting a story of resilience and hope. So, as you turn each page of your journey, remember that growth often comes quietly, through the simple act of turning the page on the past and embracing the narrative of the now.

Remember, if you're feeling anxious or down, turn to the bible or books that resonate with your situation. For example, job's story shows us how to navigate depression with faith, and jesus' time in gethsemane teaches us how to deal with anxiety by turning to god. Let these stories remind you that you're not alone and that each step, each page you turn, brings you closer to understanding and overcoming your challenges.

Putting feet on your faith means actively engaging in practices that fortify your spirit and resolve. It's about putting in the effort, knowing that while miracles happen, they often require us to meet them halfway. The transformation into a precious pearl doesn't happen overnight—it takes time, patience, and a lot of covering by god's grace.

So, dear reader, as you absorb these words and reflect on your own journey, remember that each challenge is an opportunity to grow, to evolve, and to step further into the brilliant light of understanding and faith.

IDENTITY CHECK:

Quote to Reflect:

"Reading isn't just for escape; it's a conversation with your future self."

ACTIONS TO TAKE

1. REFLECT AND WRITE
- List three lessons you've learned this year about self-worth. How have these insights shaped you?

2. ESTABLISH BOUNDARIES
- Identify one toxic trait or relationship you need to distance from. Define clear boundaries to enhance your emotional health.

3. DAILY AFFIRMATION

- Choose a meaningful affirmation or scripture, like Psalm 139:14: *"I am fearfully and wonderfully made."*

- Repeat it daily to reinforce a positive mindset.

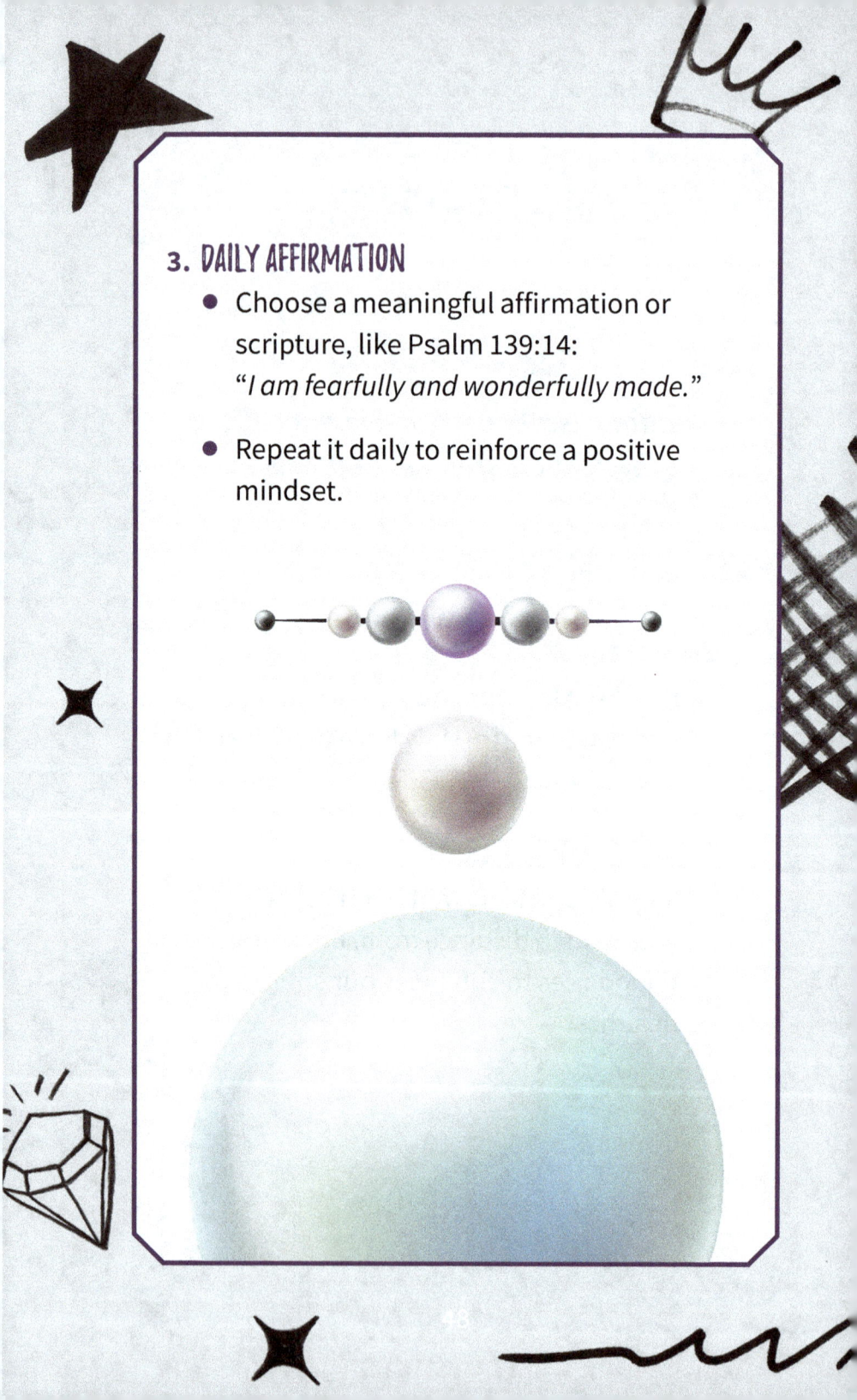

CHAPTER 5:

The Right Community

It's crucial to realize that you're the sum total of the people you surround yourself with. They reflect your values and hint at your future direction. As God unfolds the blueprint of who you are, He'll also introduce you to your tribe—the people destined to walk this path with you.

In a whirlwind of change, where the old familiar faces started to fade away, I discovered something vital: growth often means outgrowing. It can sting, yes, but it also makes room for new relationships that feel as though they were hand-picked by God just for you.

Take Joshua's Journey, for instance. It started as a youth group but quickly evolved into a pivotal connection point. One fine dining night at Oceanaire Seafood Room in downtown Baltimore transformed casual acquaintances into a tight-knit circle of friends. We didn't just share a meal; we shared our aspirations, laughed over past faux pas, and planned future adventures together. When it turned out none of us had roommates for the upcoming spa retreat, it was a no-brainer to team up.

Our bond solidified on the ride home with Destinee, one of the girls. As we chatted, our connection deepened with every topic we covered. By the time she hopped out of the car, a new group chat buzzed with messages, sealing our newfound friendship.

This group became a daily touchstone. We shared everything from mundane day-to-day updates to deep spiritual struggles. We supported each other in ways I had only hoped for in friendships. Being around them was refreshing—they got it. They understood the walk, the faith, without needing any explanation.

But then, a test. A breakup text from a long-time friend shook me to my core. I was surrounded by my new tribe when the message came, and the pain was palpable. Yet, the support I received was immediate and heartfelt. We gathered in a circle, hands clasped tightly, voices lifted in prayer. The comfort I felt from their words and presence was a balm to my troubled heart.

As I drove home later, tears mixed with reflections on the importance of the right community. Letting go of past relationships to embrace new ones wasn't just necessary; it was divinely orchestrated. God was pruning my circle, teaching me to release what no longer served my growth to make room for relationships that would.

Jeremiah 29:11 echoed in my thoughts as I navigated the quiet streets: "For I know the plans I have for you, declares the Lord, plans for welfare and not for evil, to give you a future and a hope." This scripture wasn't just comforting; it was a directive. God doesn't randomly shuffle people in and out of our lives; He strategically places each person to play a pivotal role in our spiritual journey and personal growth.

One thing I learned in my process is don't hold on to what God is telling you to let go of. If God is telling you to let go of something, it's because He has something better. It may sound cliché but it's true. As much as I wanted to talk about mending our friendship, I had to realize this was a God thing; one friend went and He placed three people in her place. You see how that works? When we are obedient to what God says, even if it doesn't feel good, it works for our good. God is intentional. I went from a friendship that was cool but I was the only one really trying to serve God, to friendships where we served God with one another. After putting it in that perspective, letting go became easier and I embraced the new relationships I was building. With the friends God had picked out for me, I finally felt I had a sense of belonging. From the girl that felt like she didn't fit in with anyone to now feeling like I finally have a place where people understand who I really was, it was definitely a prayer answered by God.

Here's a lesson straight from your big sis in faith: The company you keep can elevate you or hold you back. It's essential to be mindful of who you let into your inner circle because they influence your thoughts, actions, and decisions. As you grow and evolve, your friendships should too. They should reflect who you are becoming, not just who you were.

So, as you step into your own identity, remember that God doesn't just reveal your purpose; He reveals your people. The right community isn't just where you fit; it's where you flourish. Embrace the changes, lean into new relationships, and always move forward with a tribe that uplifts you. True friends aren't just there for the fun times; they are the warriors by your side through every battle, cheering you on, praying with you, and reminding you of who you are in Christ. Because with the right people by your side, every step forward is a step toward a brighter, more fulfilling destiny.

IDENTITY CHECK:

Quote:

"Looking back and holding on to things that no longer serves us only hurts us in the end, it can create more emotional pain, drama and prolongs our process."

1. Is there anything that God is telling you to let go of?

2. If so, are you still holding on to it?

3. If your answer is yes, why?

CHAPTER 6:

Truly A Part of the Church-Your Voice, There's Power

Life began to stabilize. I was nestled comfortably in steady friendships, actively involved in various church ministries, and my relationship with God was flourishing. I wasn't just another face in the pews; I was an integral part of a community where I could serve and connect with others who shared my passion for faith. It felt like I had finally found my tribe, a group where I could truly be myself and grow spiritually.

Yet, one pesky issue remained unresolved—the custody case that seemed to drag on endlessly. As it lingered, my approach to handling it evolved. Inspired by a strategy from my counselor, I proposed three different visitation schedules to demonstrate my willingness to compromise—a tactic appreciated by legal professionals and aimed at smoothing the proceedings.

The day of the settlement court approached, and I felt a mix of anticipation and nerves. It could all end here, or we might be pushed to a trial. My mornings were spent in prayer and meditation, seeking God's peace and preparing myself for whatever the day held. My lawyer and I were the first to arrive at court, where he asked me to prioritize my proposed visitation schedules. The other party soon joined, and negotiations began.

Surprisingly, the talks were less tense than I expected. With each passing minute, my anxiety eased, replaced by a serene confidence. After some back and forth, we reached an agreement based on my preferred option. Relief washed over me as we concluded without needing a judge's intervention. I remember walking out of the courtroom, a smile spreading across my face, feeling lighter than I had in months.

On my way home, I couldn't help but reflect on the journey. From the day the case started to the moment it ended, it had taken nine long months—a period as significant as the gestation of a new life. This wasn't just a legal battle; it was a transformative experience that had birthed a new me. This ordeal had taught me to assert myself, to use my voice with confidence and clarity.

The Bible speaks of Esther, a queen who used her voice to alter the fate of her people. Her courageous appeal to the king spared her people from annihilation. Like Esther, I learned that my voice had the power to change outcomes. It could advocate for justice, initiate new beginnings, and even save lives. This revelation was profound and empowering.

As I settled into the comfort of my home that evening, I felt a deep connection with God. I realized that every struggle, every challenge was a lesson in disguise. The custody ordeal had taught me more than just legal strategy; it had taught me about personal strength and the undeniable power of a spoken word.

Through this process, God had shown me that no matter the length of the trial, He is meticulously crafting our character, refining us like pearls. And just as a pearl is formed through irritation and time, our trials shape us into beings of resilience and beauty.

This chapter of my life closed with a newfound understanding of my voice's power and a vision to empower others, especially young girls who might be struggling to find their own voices. Inspired, I began to lay the groundwork for a mentoring program that would equip them with the courage to speak up and the wisdom to use their voices wisely.

Remember, your voice is a divine tool, endowed with the power to change your world. Use it wisely, boldly, and with the faith that it can indeed move mountains.

IDENTITY CHECK:

Quote:

"Use your voice, your voice has power."

1. REFLECT

Is there a situation in your life where you need to speak up? What's holding you back?

2. EXPLORE

Identify what fears or concerns are preventing you from using your voice effectively.

3. ACTION

Dive into the Book of Esther. See how Esther's courage to speak changed the destiny of her people. What can you learn from her example that might apply to your situation?

CHAPTER 7:

Lessons in Letting Go and Holding On

If there's one truth that resonates deeply with me, it's this: growth is often accompanied by the subtle temptation to revert to old habits that subtly hinder us. After navigating through the visible battles and finding what seemed like peace, I mistakenly thought it was safe to ease up on my spiritual disciplines. This lapse, however, left me unexpectedly vulnerable, opening the door to more turmoil than I had anticipated.

In the wake of the custody battle's conclusion, there was a deceptive sense of closure that led me to believe I could relax the stringent routines that had steadied me through storms. It felt like a breath of fresh air to reclaim weekends and reconnect with old friends, engaging in the carefree joys that had been sidelined by court dates and parenting schedules. Yet, this shift, while refreshing, slowly unmoored me from the practices that kept my spirit attuned to God's voice.

As my involvement in church and daily devotionals waned, so did the strength of my spiritual armor. It was during this time of relaxed vigilance that I reconnected with Antonio, an old college acquaintance. Our renewed friendship quickly blossomed into something more, and as it did, my priorities shifted dramatically. Antonio, with his easy charm and renewed presence in my life, unintentionally encouraged my drift from disciplined faith to a more secular lifestyle.

The return of legal challenges served as a harsh reminder of my vulnerability. This time, the complications were not just mine to bear; Antonio was swept into the ensuing chaos, complicating our lives further and testing the resilience of our budding relationship. The legal entanglements, stressful and draining, were compounded by my spiritual negligence, creating a perfect storm of personal and relational trials.

One particularly sobering moment came with the repossession of my car—a jarring, tangible sign of how far things had spiraled out of control. This setback forced me to confront the consequences of my choices head-on. It was a painful but necessary wake-up call that realigned my focus from the temporal to the eternal. I found myself returning to prayer, not out of ritual but from a deep-seated need for divine intervention.

During this reflective time, Antonio and I started to seek solace in our faith, attending church more regularly and engaging with a community that reminded us of God's constant presence and promises. This spiritual reconnection did not erase our problems but gave us the strength to face them together. It taught us the value of unity and spiritual support in overcoming life's hurdles.

The journey through these trials underscored a pivotal lesson: our spiritual growth must be guarded zealously, especially when it seems we've reached a safe harbor. The temptation to ease up on our spiritual disciplines can lead to vulnerabilities that are only revealed when new storms hit. Each setback, while painful, brought invaluable lessons about the importance of maintaining my spiritual health with the same diligence I applied to resolving my external challenges.

Reflecting on this season of my life, I see it not only as a narrative of personal struggle but as a testament to the necessity of continuous spiritual vigilance. The ebb and flow of life's challenges are not merely obstacles but opportunities to reinforce our faith and refine our character.

This chapter of my life, shared with you now, serves as both a caution and an encouragement: hold fast to the disciplines that anchor you in faith, no matter the season. Embrace the growth, resist the urge to revert to old ways, and know that each step, whether forward or seemingly backward, is guided by a God who uses every circumstance for our ultimate good and His glory.

IDENTITY CHECK:

Quote:

"Hold fast to the disciplines that anchor you in faith, no matter the season."

1. **REFLECTION:**

   Can you identify a time when easing up on your spiritual or personal disciplines led to unexpected challenges? Describe that period and what you learned from it.

2. **ASSESSMENT:**

   What are some practices or habits that you need to reintegrate or strengthen in your life to maintain your growth and resilience against life's challenges?

3. **COMMITMENT:**

   Choose one spiritual discipline (such as prayer, fasting, studying scripture, or regular church attendance) to focus on strengthening over the next month. Write

down specific steps you will take to incorporate this discipline more consistently into your daily routine.

4. **CONNECTION:**
   How can you ensure that your spiritual growth is supported by the right community? List ways you can engage more with supportive friends or groups that align with your values and growth goals.

This identity check is designed to help you reflect on your vulnerabilities and reinforce your commitments, ensuring that you are better equipped to handle the ups and downs of life while staying true to your core values and beliefs.

CHAPTER 8:

Invitation to Discover Me

Amidst the lingering court battles and the daily grind, a profound shift was taking place in my life. It was during these trying times that I truly began to hear God's voice, steering me away from the forefront of turmoil and toward a deeper discovery of myself. This chapter of my life wasn't just about legal struggles; it was about shedding the superficial layers and grappling with my spiritual identity.

One afternoon, a routine scroll through Facebook led me to a live session that would pivot my spiritual journey. The speaker discussed how the enemy schemes to steal our identities, ensuring we never grasp who we truly are or attain our God-given purposes. It resonated deeply as she detailed the tactics used to ensnare us, particularly through spirits of rejection and abandonment.

The spirit of rejection, she explained, leaves one feeling overlooked and unworthy, constantly seeking approval and fearing rejection. This spirit skews our perception of God's love, making us feel undeserving of His grace. Then there's the spirit of abandonment, which often partners with rejection. It breeds a tendency to linger in detrimental relationships, fosters isolation, and stems from deep-seated emotional voids rooted in early life experiences.

As I absorbed her words, I realized these spirits were manifestations of the "orphan spirit" — a condition characterized by feelings of resentment, comparison, and anger. This was a revelation. My life, from feeling perpetually out of place to my relentless quest for validation, mirrored the orphan spirit's influence. Even as a child, during my parents' tumultuous divorce, the seeds of rejection and abandonment were sown. When my mother, in a moment of overwhelming distress, expelled my brother and me from our home, those seeds took root.

This episode wasn't just a childhood ordeal; it was the onset of a pattern that shadowed me into adulthood. My father's broken promises further entrenched these feelings. His absence and unreliability, especially during critical moments like my failed attempt to attend senior prom, underscored a painful lesson in self-reliance and mistrust.

Reflecting on these experiences, I understood that my difficulties in forming deep, trusting relationships stemmed from this ingrained orphan spirit. Despite growing up surrounded by family, I never truly felt I belonged. My views on God and confrontation clashed with my family's more passive stances, deepening my sense of isolation.

The Facebook live session was more than an eye-opener; it was a call to action. The speaker's passion for God's truth urged me to seek my true identity in Christ, to shed the orphan spirit, and embrace the spirit of adoption. It was clear that performing religious rituals wasn't enough. I needed a genuine connection with Christ to uncover the person He intended me to be.

This realization marked the beginning of a deeper journey with Christ. It wasn't just about fighting against what was wrong in my life but about embracing and understanding my rightful place in God's kingdom. Understanding our spiritual identity is not merely about overcoming external battles but about internal transformation. This journey taught me that discovering our identity in Christ is essential for spiritual maturity and enduring peace. It's about embracing the truth of who we are in Him, free from the enemy's distortions and fully alive to God's purposeful design for our lives.

CHAPTER 9:

Discovering Who God Says I Am

After tuning into the Hour of Power, I was taken aback by how little I truly understood about my identity in Christ. Despite my diligent scripture reading and prayer, I realized I was battling spiritual influences whose names and impacts were previously unknown to me. The message I heard that day catapulted me into a deep dive, exploring various spirits and their characteristics, to uncover any unseen forces at play in my life.

This revelation marked the beginning of an essential journey: discovering who God declares I am. It prompted a fundamental question—Who is God? Knowing someone's character is crucial to truly identifying with them. I embarked on this exploration with a Bible plan titled "Who is God?" which unfolded over 23 days. Each day, the plan revealed different attributes of God—His love, forgiveness, creativity, fatherly nature, and holiness, to name a few. As I progressed through the plan, I began to recognize these attributes manifesting in various aspects of my life, deepening my understanding of God's presence and work in my experiences.

Upon completing the Bible plan, I delved into the Scriptures to discover how God described Himself. One statement that particularly resonated with me was God's declaration to Moses, "I am who I am." This simple yet profound assertion captured the essence of God's eternal and unchangeable nature, sparking both amusement and awe within me. To further grasp His complexities, I studied the various names of God—Elohim, Jehovah Rapha, Jehovah Gibbor, Jehovah Shalom, and Jehovah Jireh, among others. Each name revealed a different aspect of God's capacity to meet us in our needs—whether as a healer, a mighty warrior, a source of peace, or our provider. This rich tapestry of names helped paint a more comprehensive picture of God's character, providing comfort and reassurance that He could be whatever I needed in any circumstance.

Armed with a deeper understanding of God's multifaceted nature, I turned to Scripture to see how God viewed me. The journey began with Genesis 1:27, which states, "So God created human beings in His own image. In the image of God, He created them; male and female He created them." This verse was foundational, affirming that like God, I am imbued with qualities of love, patience, and creativity. As I reflected on this, I realized that being made in God's image meant that I too am inherently good and worthy.

Further exploration led me to Psalm 139:14-16, which declares, "I praise you because I am fearfully and wonderfully made; your works are wonderful, I know that full well." This passage not only highlighted God's intricate work in creating me but also emphasized that I am a wonderful creation, regardless of past mistakes or how others may perceive me. The realization that I was crafted with intention and care was incredibly affirming.

Another transformative Scripture was 1 Peter 2:9, which reads, "But you are a chosen people, a royal priesthood, a holy nation, God's special possession, that you may declare the praises of him who called you out of darkness into his wonderful light." This verse shifted my perspective on self-worth, reminding me of my royal status and chosen place in God's kingdom, independent of human validation.

My journey of self-discovery didn't stop with the Bible; it also included insightful books like "From Mediocrity to Maturity" by Apostle Kadesh Jenkins. This book deepened my understanding of my royal identity, explaining the descent of the Holy Spirit as a mark of our direct lineage to God, the King. Such revelations eradicated any residual feelings of inadequacy.

Discovering who God says I am transformed my view of myself and my life's purpose. It instilled in me a profound sense of belonging and an appreciation for the unconditional love God has for me. Recognizing that I am a part of a royal priesthood and cherished by God gave me a new outlook on life, fueling my desire to live out my purpose with confidence and grace.

IDENTITY CHECK

Quote:

"But you are a chosen people, a royal priesthood, a holy nation, God's special possession, that you may declare the praises of him who called you out of darkness into his wonderful light."
—1 Peter 2:9

QUESTIONS TO PONDER:

1. IDENTIFY YOUR UNDERSTANDING:

How do you currently see yourself in relation to God? Do you view yourself as His chosen and special possession? Why or why not?

2. SCRIPTURAL REFLECTION:

Reflect on Psalm 139:14-16. Write down what it means to you to be "fearfully and wonderfully made" by God.

3. DECLARATION OF IDENTITY:

Choose one attribute of God (such as Jehovah Rapha the healer, or Jehovah Shalom the prince of peace) that you need to embrace in your life right now. How can embracing this attribute change your current circumstances or mindset?

4. ACTION STEP:

Spend time in prayer each day this week, asking God to help you see yourself as He sees you—chosen, loved, and valuable. Write down any revelations or encouraging thoughts that come during this time.

CHAPTER 10:

Embrace Who I Am

Discovering my identity in Christ marked the beginning of a profound transformation, even as I faced the looming dates of my custody case. Each time I thought about the proceedings, a wave of irritation and frustration would wash over me. It seemed as if every lie told by my daughter's father was invisible to others. In those moments of despair, I clung to the powerful lessons I had learned: to use my voice and to remember who I belonged to. The knowledge I gained about the names of God, particularly the name Jehovah Roi—the God who sees—provided comfort during those trying times. I trusted that He was aware of everything and that in His perfect timing, justice would prevail for His glory.

During this season, the scripture, "For we walk by faith, not by sight" (2 Corinthians 5:7), became my anchor. I would repeat it, embedding it deep within my heart, striving to view my situation through the lens of faith rather than fear. However, frustration often seemed to have the upper hand, prompting me to delve deeper into understanding its roots. I discovered that such emotions are often tied to underlying fears. When frustration mounts, it's beneficial to write down your specific frustrations, identify any associated fears, and then surrender them to God.

Here's how I approached it through prayer:

Prayer: *"Lord, this court case is frustrating me because it seems my child's father manipulates the truth, and I fear the judge might rule in his favor despite his dishonesty. Your Word tells me to cast all my cares upon You because You care for me (1 Peter 5:7). I lay this burden at Your feet, trusting You to work for Your glory. In Jesus' name, Amen."*

This act of praying and reminding God of His promises demonstrates faith and is encouraged by scriptures like Isaiah 43:26, where God invites us to present our case to Him. It's crucial to trust in God's timing and not to reclaim the worries we've handed over to Him. If you find it challenging to let go, continue to seek God's guidance on what may be hindering your trust.

Embracing who I am in Christ means approaching God with the confidence of a child, as stated in 1 John 3:1: "See what great love the Father has lavished on us, that we should be called children of God! And that is what we are!" Another verse that fortified my identity during this time was 1 John 4:4, "You, dear children, are from God and have overcome them, because the one who is in you is greater than the one who is in the world." Realizing the magnitude of God's power within me—a power that overcame death and can perform miracles—was transformative.

I had known these truths early in my faith journey, but they never resonated as deeply as they did during this challenging period. Understanding that I am a child of God, a co-heir with Christ, and a member of a royal priesthood made in God's image helped me not only to endure but to thrive in the midst of trials. Just like me, you are not defined by your circumstances. With God, you have the power to overcome them.

CHAPTER 11:

God speaks

The culmination of my custody battle marked a profound moment of revelation and affirmation. As I stood on the precipice of potentially tumultuous court proceedings, I realized the depth of what I had learned about God and myself. It was not merely about the legal battle but about the spiritual revelation of identity and the power inherent in knowing who I was in Christ.

On the first day of the trial, as I entered the courtroom, a serene calm enveloped me, despite the storm of emotions swirling around. This serenity was not born out of naivety but from a deep-seated knowledge of God's character and His promises. Throughout my journey, I had come to know God as Jehovah Rapha, the Healer; Jehovah Gibbor, the Mighty Warrior; and

Jehovah Shalom, the Prince of Peace. Each name not only described His capabilities but also His promises to me, His child.

The courtroom was fraught with tension, my daughter's father and his lawyer exuding a confidence that seemed unshakeable. Yet, in that moment of potential intimidation, God reminded me of His promise in Exodus 14:14, "The Lord will fight for you; you need only to be still." This divine whisper was a call to embrace the identity He had revealed to me — an identity rooted in power, not passivity; in divine right, not human might.

As the proceedings unfolded, and as I listened to the fabrications and boasts from the other side, a scripture anchored my resolve: "But you are a chosen people, a royal priesthood, a holy nation, God's special possession..." (1 Peter 2:9). This passage reminded me that my battle was not merely legal but spiritual, and my victory was assured not by human judges but by divine decree.

The turning point came when God prompted me to recall a crucial piece of evidence — a text message that could substantiate my claims. This wasn't just a reminder of a forgotten message; it was a testament to God's intimate involvement in our lives. He speaks, sometimes in whispers that echo through our memories, guiding us to truths we might have overlooked.

As I presented this evidence to my lawyer, the atmosphere shifted. What seemed like an insurmountable pride from the opposing side began to deflate. The judge's decision to encourage a settlement rather than proceed with the trial was a clear manifestation of God working behind the scenes. My voice was never raised in defense; my identity in Christ spoke louder than words could.

This experience underscored a crucial lesson: knowing who you are in Christ transforms how you face battles. It's not about the noise and clamor of the fight; it's about the quiet confidence that comes from understanding your divine backing. As the trial concluded, not only was the legal matter settled, but a greater truth was cemented in my heart — I am His child, chosen, seen, and defended.

For every reader grappling with battles that seem beyond your control, remember this: your identity in God is the cornerstone of your victory. The trials you face do not define you; they refine you. They are opportunities for God to demonstrate His power and for you to experience His faithfulness. In the grand narrative of your life, let your identity in Christ be the anchor that steadies you, the wisdom that guides you, and the victory that defines you.

IDENTITY CHECK: HEARING GOD'S VOICE IN THE SILENCE

REFLECTION:

Do you recognize the moments when God is speaking up for you? Sometimes His interventions are not loud or visible. Reflect on a time when you felt God subtly but powerfully making a way for you.

SCRIPTURE MEDITATION:

Meditate on Exodus 14:14, "The Lord will fight for you; you need only to be still." How can you apply this promise to your current challenges?

JOURNAL PROMPT:

Write about a situation where you need God to speak or act on your behalf. How can understanding your identity in Christ change your perspective on this situation?

ACTION STEP:

Identify a fear or concern you're facing and write it down. Next to it, write a declaration of faith based on who God says He is and who He says you are. For example, if you're worried about a decision, declare, "God is my wisdom; I am guided by His hand."

PRAYER:

Spend time praying, asking God to make His presence and voice clearer in your life. Ask for the faith to be still and know that He is God, especially in times when you're tempted to take matters into your own hands.

CHAPTER 12:

I Am His Child

Imagine you're standing at a crossroads, much like I did during my tumultuous custody battle. Here, at this junction, you face decisions that might feel overwhelming, and it seems like every path is shrouded in uncertainty. But what if I told you that the key to navigating this maze isn't just about choosing the right path but understanding who walks with you and who you truly are?

You see, during my court trials, there was more at play than legal strategies or the quest for justice. It was a profound journey of self-discovery and spiritual awakening. It was about recognizing that beyond the earthly courts, there's a divine court where I am seen, known, and loved unconditionally. This realization isn't just my story; it's an invitation to you as well.

Let's talk about your battles—the ones that push you to the brink of despair, the ones that seem unfair and unending. Have you ever felt like giving up when no one seems to understand or see your struggle? In those moments, remember, you are not hidden from view. You are in the sightline of Jehovah Roi, the God who sees everything. He's not just a passive observer; He's actively involved, ready to intervene on your behalf.

Think about the names of God I learned to cling to in my darkest hours: Jehovah Rapha, your healer; Jehovah Gibbor, mighty in battle; Elohim, supreme and mighty. These names aren't just ancient titles; they are promises of His presence and power in your life. When you feel overwhelmed by the storms, remember Jonah. God didn't just observe his struggle; He provided a way out at the right time. This same God is navigating your storms too.

But here's the crucial part: understanding your identity in Him. You are created in His image—crafted with precision, designed with purpose, and cherished beyond measure. When you grasp this truth, the lies of inadequacy, fear, and doubt start losing their grip.

You are not the sum of your past mistakes or the labels others have placed on you. You are fearfully and wonderfully made, a royal priesthood, a holy nation, God's special possession.

Let this truth sink in: You are chosen. Even if the world overlooks you, even if you feel forgotten in the back rows of life's theater, you hold a VIP pass in the kingdom of heaven. You are not just a face in the crowd; you are a child of the King.

So, as you face your own battles, don't just focus on the challenge itself but on the powerful ally you have in God. Invite Him into your struggles, let Him speak for you when you're too weary to fight, and watch as He turns what seems like your end into a new beginning.

Your story isn't just about overcoming obstacles; it's about discovering and claiming your identity in Christ. Each chapter of your life, each challenge you face, is a stepping stone towards this profound truth. So, walk confidently, armed with the knowledge of who you are in Him, and let this identity shape every decision, every battle, and every victory.

As you turn the pages of your life, remember the ultimate lesson from my journey: With God, you are always more than enough. Embrace who you are in Him, and let this truth empower you to rise above every challenge with grace and strength.

CHAPTER 13:

A Daughter With A Destiny

Throughout my life, battles have shaped me, many waged in silent corners of my existence. These deep-rooted battles, fought quietly, became shadows that molded my worldview and, critically, my self-perception. I grappled with generational struggles that followed me into adulthood, often feeling lost in their midst. Yet, it was through the 'But God' moments during my custody trials that I began to see clearly who I was meant to be, helping me to rise as the daughter destined for more.

Reflecting on the series of trials and court cases, I realized there were actually two daughters on trial. While I fought for my daughter's well-being, God was championing His own—me. This revelation was profound: in every challenge, God introduces us to our destiny, refining us through life's fires to emerge as daughters of strength and purpose.

During these trials, as I stood advocating for my daughter, God stood advocating for me. He used these moments not just to resolve a legal matter but to reveal a deeper truth about identity and belonging. I learned that to truly step into the destiny God had for me, I had to shed the false identities—the ones shaped by unfavorable family dynamics, rejection, and a lack of boundaries.

God showed me that knowing Him was the key to understanding myself. As I delved deeper into His character—discovering Him as Jehovah Roi, who sees me; Jehovah Gibbor, who fights for me; and Elohim, the sovereign over my life—I began to see reflections of His image in myself. These names of God were not just theological concepts but real, active roles He played in my life story.

The journey to embracing my true identity was also a journey of letting go. I had to relinquish the narratives handed down through generations, the ones that no longer served me or aligned with the truth of who I was in Christ. This process was not without pain; it involved confronting and setting boundaries with loved ones, which often resulted in misunderstandings and emotional distance.

Yet, this distancing was necessary for healing. It allowed me to break free from cycles of comparison and colorism that had plagued my family for generations. In establishing boundaries, I was not just protecting myself but also paving a new path for my children—one where they could grow up understanding their inherent worth and divine heritage without the shadows of past insecurities.

As I stood firm in my new identity, God brought clarity and healing. The name change after my marriage marked a significant turning point. Shifting from Jessica Jenkins to Jessica Hardy wasn't just a formal requirement; it was a prophetic act. 'Hardy,' meaning bold, contrasted starkly with 'Jenkins,' derived from 'little John.' This change was symbolic of the transformation God had wrought in me—from shrinking in the background to standing bold and confident in my calling.

In embracing my new name, I was also claiming the territory God had prepared for me. It became clear that to occupy the spaces God opens up, we must fully embrace the identity He gives. It's about owning who we are in Him—bold, chosen, and destined for impact.

This book, then, is more than a recounting of trials and victories; it's an invitation to you, the reader, to discover and embrace your identity as God's beloved daughter. It's a call to move beyond the labels and limitations imposed by others and to step into the fullness of what God has ordained for you.

As we close this chapter, remember that your identity is not just a label—it's a legacy. It connects you to a divine purpose that transcends your circumstances and equips you to overcome. You are not just surviving; you are thriving as a daughter of destiny, called to manifest heaven's plans on earth. Embrace this truth, and watch as every area of your life aligns with the glorious destiny God has in store for you.

EPILOGUE:

Embracing Your PEARL Identity

As we draw to the close of this journey, I invite you to reflect on the pearls of wisdom woven through each chapter, guiding us towards a deeper understanding of our true selves. This book, "*Identify Her: Pearls of Wisdom for the Young Adult Finding Purpose,*" is more than a narrative of trials and triumphs; it's a beacon for all who are navigating the waters of identity and purpose.

The PEARL framework of this book encapsulates the essence of our shared journey:

P - PRAYER:

Throughout each challenge and victory, the power of prayer stood as our foundational tool. It is through prayer that we communicate with God, lay down our burdens, and strengthen our faith. As you move forward, let prayer be your first response, not your last resort.

E - EMBRACE:

Embracing your identity in Christ is crucial. As illustrated through my own experiences, understanding who you are in God paves the way for all other aspects of your life to align with His purpose. Embrace your identity as God's chosen, loved, and empowered child.

A - AWARENESS:

Awareness of God's presence and His promises has been a constant theme. Recognizing His sovereignty in every situation helps us to navigate life with confidence and peace. Stay aware of His nearness and His desire to lead you into all truth and wisdom.

R - RESILIENCE:

The stories shared here are testaments to the resilience that is birthed through faith. Each trial you face is not just an obstacle but an opportunity to grow stronger and more anchored in your faith. Resilience is built through overcoming, and with God, you are more than a conqueror.

L - LEGACY:

Finally, understanding that your journey is about leaving a legacy that glorifies God. Your life is a testament to His grace, and your story will inspire others to seek their own relationship with Him. As you live out your purpose, remember that you are setting a foundation for generations to come.

As you step out from the pages of this book and into the reality of your daily life, carry these pearls with you. Let them remind you of the strength you possess and the divine strategy at your disposal. The journey of self-discovery is ongoing, and as you continue to seek God, He will reveal more of who you are meant to be.

This book is your beginning, not your conclusion. May you find in each day new reasons to pursue your God-given purpose with passion and perseverance. May you see every challenge as a stepping stone and every victory as a reminder of God's faithfulness.

Thank you for walking this path with me. Now, go forth and shine as the precious pearl you are, beautifully crafted by God, ready to make a significant impact in the world. Identify her, embrace her, and celebrate her: she is you, wonderfully made and destined for greatness.

About The Author

Jessica Hardy is a wife, mother of three wonderful children and a first time author. She is a Maryland native that had spent many years trying to figure out her purpose in life to realize her purpose would be unlocked when she found out her true identity is in Christ. She has worked in government for 10 years and realized

Her passion is to help the next generation to positively identify who they are so they can boldly walk into their purpose through mentoring.

SPEAK. EQUIPT. INSPIRE
PARTNER WITH JESSICA

The founder of THE PEARLS ©framework, and mentor to young women worldwide, Jessica has made it a point to share her wisdom and experiences in a real and relatable way by inspiring young women to find their authentic selves in a society where superficial attributes are praised. Jessica's real and relatable nature captivates her audiences and inspires real change and confidence.

**HIRE JESSICA TO SPEAK, TRAIN, OR HOST
YOUR NEXT EVENT**

HIRE JESSICA TO SPEAK, TRAIN, OR EQUIP YOUR WOMEN'S OR YOUNG GIRLS' GROUP TODAY

Jessica Hardy is a dynamic speaker and mentor who is passionate about empowering women and young girls to discover their true identity and walk confidently in their purpose. Drawing from her own transformative experiences and deep spiritual insights, Jessica offers engaging, empowering, and educational talks designed to inspire and equip. Below are two of her signature talks:

1. SIGNATURE TALK 1: UNVEILING YOUR PEARL- DISCOVERING YOUR IDENTITY IN CHRISTS

- **Description:**
  This talk encourages young girls and women to peel back the layers of societal expectations, personal insecurities, and past hurts to reveal their true identity in Christ. Jessica uses her personal journey and biblical principles to guide participants toward a

profound understanding of who they are in God.

- **Audience:**
Best for young girls' groups, women's ministries, and Christian conferences looking to deepen their spiritual identity and self-awareness.

- **Benefits:**
  - Gain a deeper understanding of one's spiritual identity and divine purpose.
  - Learn practical steps to overcome common struggles with self-esteem and identity.
  - Be inspired to embrace one's unique gifts and callings in Christ.

2. SIGNATURE TALK 2: PEARLS OF WISDOM: NAVIGATING LIFE'S TRIALS WITH GRACE AND STRENGTH

- **Description:**

  In this empowering session, Jessica shares insights on how to transform life's challenges into opportunities for growth and testimony, much like how pearls are formed through irritation and pressure. Participants will learn to apply biblical wisdom and practical strategies to handle life's challenges more effectively.

  - *Audience:* Ideal for women's retreats, youth empowerment workshops, and church groups seeking to equip their members with resilience and spiritual maturity.

- **Benefits:**

  - Understand the biblical perspective on suffering and trials.
  - Develop resilience and the ability to see God's hand in challenging circumstances.
  - Encourage a community of support and shared growth among participants.

CONTACT INFORMATION
TO BOOK JESSICA

Email:
jessicatheauthor@gmail.com
Email:
jessica@thejessicahardy.com

Invite Jessica to your next event and witness a transformational shift in the lives of your participants as they learn to identify and embrace their God-given destinies.

www.thejessicahardy.com

www.ingramcontent.com/pod-product-compliance
Lightning Source LLC
Chambersburg PA
CBHW060336130626
46553CB00003B/1016